VEGETARIAN
FOR
ONE AND TWO

PARRAGON

VEGETARIAN
FOR
ONE AND TWO

Photography by Peter Barry
Designed by Claire Leighton and
    Helen Johnson
Edited by Jillian Stewart and Kate Cranshaw

3565
© 1994 Coombe Books
This edition published 1994
for Parragon Book Service Ltd., Unit 13-17, Avonbridge Trading Estate,
Atlantic Road, Avonmouth, Bristol BS11 9QD
All rights reserved.
Printed in Hong Kong
ISBN 1-85813-583-4

Contents

Introduction

This book is about cooking small amounts of vegetarian food for just one or two people, and is aimed at those living on their own, vegetarian couples, and for those who are cooking an extra vegetarian dish for a member of the family or a friend who has opted for a vegetarian diet.

Many people feel that if they embrace a vegetarian diet, they are contributing not only to their own good health – and it has been proved that vegetarians generally have less heart disease, less intestinal disorders and better teeth – but also to a gentler, more rational, and more ecologically sound world. The market has responded handsomely to the trend towards vegetarianism. Our supermarkets are bursting at the seams with excellent quality fruit and vegetables from all over the world. The choice of dairy products has also increased dramatically over the past decades, with great emphasis being given to the low-fat varieties of yogurt and vegetarian cheese. Supermarkets and healthfood shops now store an array of grains such as flours, rices, couscous, bulgar, oats, and pulses such as lentils, kidney beans, haricot beans and chick peas, as well as soya-bean derivatives such as bean curd, smoked bean curd, soya milks and soya sauces. The choice of vegetarian foods has never been greater nor the variety more stimulating.

There are certain aspects of our high-tech modern world that actually make it far easier to shop and cook for one or two than ever it was before. Electronic tills in the shops enable the shopper to buy small amounts, such as two or three items of fruit, or a single head of broccoli, a couple of tomatoes, or whatever, without incurring the shopkeeper's wrath. Also, once home with the shopping, the microwave can be of tremendous help, particularly when cooking vegetables and reheating dishes made previously. Of course, the freezer, too, has obvious advantages when dealing with small quantities. Delicious soups and casseroles can be made, divided into single portions and frozen for later use.

People cooking small amounts generally do not want to spend too long preparing meals, and that is what this book is all about. The recipes are easy to follow and each one has an extra ingredient or clever method to make the dish particularly appetising. For instance, potatoes are stuffed with watercress, and grapefruit is served hot and spicy. Also, there are many dishes that could be served alongside equivalent meat dishes for when only one or two round the table are vegetarian, such as Vegetarian Shepherd's Pie, Savoury Bean Pot, Sweet Bean Curry and Vegetable Cassoulet. In this way the same accompanying vegetables or rice can be offered to everyone. The recipes here demonstrate how cooking for vegetarians need never be a chore, and illustrate the wide and tempting spectrum of easy-to-prepare foods that vegetarianism embraces.

FRENCH ONION SOUP

This soup tastes best if cooked the day before it is needed and then reheated as required.

SERVES 2

2 medium onions
30g/1oz butter or vegetable margarine
15g/½oz plain flour or soya flour
490ml/17 fl oz boiling vegetable stock or
    water plus 1 stock cube
Salt and pepper

Topping
2 slices French bread, cut crosswise
45g/1½oz vegetarian Cheddar cheese,
    grated

1. Slice the onions very finely into rings.

2. Melt the butter or margarine in a pan, add the onion rings and sauté over a medium heat until well browned.

3. Mix in the flour and stir well until browned.

4. Gradually stir in the stock and add some seasoning. Bring to the boil, reduce the heat and simmer for 30 minutes.

5. Toast the bread on both sides then top with the cheese, and grill until golden brown and melted.

6. Place the slices of bread and cheese in the bottom of individual soup dishes and spoon the soup over the top. Serve at once.

TIME: Preparation takes 10 minutes, cooking takes about 40 minutes.

VARIATION: For a special occasion, add a tablespoonful of brandy to the stock.

WATCHPOINT: The onions must be very well browned, as this gives the rich colour to the soup.

CORN OYSTERS

These tasty fritters are very versatile and can also be eaten as a snack or as an accompaniment to a main course.

SERVES 2

225g/8oz sweetcorn
1 tbsp flour
Pinch of salt, pepper and sugar
1 egg, separated
Butter or oil, for frying
2 spring onions, finely chopped
Parsley, to garnish

1. Mash the sweetcorn to break it up slightly, but do not purée it. Mix in the flour, salt, pepper and sugar.

2. Beat the egg yolk until thick and pale lemon coloured and combine with the corn. Beat the egg white until stiff peaks form and fold into the corn mixture.

3. Heat a small amount of butter or oil in a frying pan and when hot, drop in tablespoons of the corn mixture.

4. Cook for a few minutes until risen and brown then turn over and cook the second side until golden.

5. Serve sprinkled with chopped spring onions, garnish with sprigs of parsley and accompany with pepper relish.

TIME: Preparation takes about 15 minutes and cooking takes about 5-6 minutes per batch.

COOK'S TIP: Make sure you add a good pinch of salt to the batter and cook the fritters in batches, to avoid overcrowding the pan.

VARIATION: Use the same quantity of other vegetables such as carrots or parsnips, that have been cooked, drained and diced. Add a little cayenne pepper or crushed dried chillies to make a spicy variation.

CREAM OF CARROT SOUP

This is a classic soup which is suitable for any occasion.

SERVES 2

1 small onion, chopped
1 clove garlic, crushed
2 tsps olive oil
225g/½lb carrots, chopped
½ tsp mixed herbs
420ml/¾ pint stock
60ml/4 tbsps soured cream
Salt and pepper

1. Sauté the chopped onion and garlic in the oil until transparent.

2. Add the carrots, mixed herbs and stock.

3. Bring to the boil and simmer for about 30 minutes until the carrots are soft.

4. Cool a little and then liquidise until smooth.

5. Add the soured cream, season to taste and mix thoroughly.

6. Heat through gently and serve.

TIME: Preparation takes about 10 minutes, cooking takes 35 minutes.

WATCHPOINT: Do not allow the soup to boil after adding the soured cream.

VARIATION: For a richer soup, omit the soured cream and add a swirl of double cream just before serving.

AUBERGINE CAVIAR

This novel starter is an interesting and different way of serving this delicious vegetable.

SERVES 2

1 small aubergine
Salt
2 tbsps walnut oil
1 clove garlic, crushed
2 tsps lemon juice
Pinch cayenne pepper
1 egg, hard-boiled (optional)
2 tbsps finely chopped onion
2-4 slices French bread, toasted
1 tbsp chopped fresh parsley

1. Remove the stalk from the aubergine and cut in half lengthways. Using a small sharp knife, score the cut surfaces of the aubergine, at 1.25cm/½-inch intervals, in a lattice pattern.

2. Sprinkle each cut surface well with salt and leave to stand for 30 minutes, to draw out any bitterness and excess water. Rinse thoroughly and pat dry with kitchen paper.

3. Cut the aubergine into chunks. Heat the oil in a frying pan and sauté the aubergine and garlic for about 10 minutes, or until tender.

4. Place the aubergine into a food processor along with the lemon juice, cayenne and salt, and process to chop finely. Adjust the seasoning and chill thoroughly.

5. Cut the eggs in half and separate the yolks from the whites. Push the yolks through a nylon sieve. Finely chop the egg white.

6. Pile the aubergine caviar onto the French bread and top with the chopped onion, then egg white then egg yolk. Sprinkle with chopped parsley and serve.

TIME: Preparation takes about 15 minutes, plus standing. Cooking time is about 10 minutes.

VARIATION: Use a 5cm/2-inch piece of cucumber instead of the egg in this recipe, chopping this into very small dice and sprinkling with a little black pepper before using it as a garnish.

SERVING IDEAS: Serve with a side salad.

CREAM OF CUCUMBER WITH MINT

This delicious summer soup can be eaten hot or chilled and served on ice for a refreshing change.

SERVES 2

2 medium cucumbers
490ml/17 fl oz vegetable stock
Salt and freshly ground black pepper
1-2 sprigs fresh mint
140ml/¼ pint single cream
30ml/2 tbsps natural yogurt, to garnish

1. Cut one third off one of the cucumbers and chop it into small dice. Set to one side for later use. Peel the remaining two thirds and the other cucumber and roughly chop them into small pieces.

2. Put the peeled cucumber, stock and seasoning into a large saucepan. Remove the mint leaves from the sprig and add the stalks only to the pan. Bring gently to the boil, then reduce the heat and simmer gently for 25 minutes or until the cucumber is tender.

3. Remove the mint stalks from the soup and using a liquidiser or food processor, purée the soup until smooth. Return to the rinsed out pan and stir in the single cream and reserved diced cucumber. Reheat gently for about 5 minutes.

4. To serve, finely chop the mint leaves and add to the soup. Stir a spoonful of yogurt into each bowl before serving.

TIME: Preparation takes about 15 minutes, cooking time is about 30 minutes.

VARIATION: Use a mixture of half stock and half pale ale for an interesting variation.

SPICY HOT GRAPEFRUIT

This simple dish makes an ideal first course, or even a refresher between main courses.

SERVES 2

1 ruby grapefruit
½ tsp ground allspice
1 tsp caster sugar (optional)
Lemon balm or mint leaves, to decorate

1. Cut the grapefruit in half, then using a small sharp serrated knife or a grapefruit knife, cut around the edges of each half between the flesh and the pith.

2. Carefully cut down between each segment and the membrane, take hold of the central pithy core and gently twist to remove it and the membranes which have been cut away from the grapefruit segments. Remove any pips.

3. Sprinkle each grapefruit half with equal amounts of the allspice and sugar, if using. Place under a medium preheated grill for 3-4 minutes to heat through. Garnish with lemon balm or mint leaves.

TIME: Preparation takes about 15 minutes, cooking takes 3-4 minutes.

VARIATION: Sprinkle each grapefruit with ground ginger instead of the allspice and pour a teaspoon of ginger wine or sherry over each half.

PREPARATION: The grapefruit halves can be prepared well in advance. Cover closely with cling film to prevent them from drying out.

VEGETABLE SOUP

This hearty vegetable soup makes the most of traditional and unusual vegetables.

SERVES 2

2 tbsps vegetable or olive oil
1 medium carrot, diced
1 small turnip, diced
1 small leek, washed and thinly sliced
1 medium potato, scrubbed and diced
280ml/½ pint vegetable stock
225g/8oz canned plum tomatoes, chopped
1 bay leaf
¼ tsp dried savory or marjoram
30g/1oz soup pasta
Salt and freshly ground black pepper
45g/1½oz fresh or frozen sliced green beans
60g/2oz okra, trimmed and sliced
30g/1oz frozen sweetcorn niblets
30g/1oz frozen peas
2 tsps chopped parsley

1. Heat the oil in a saucepan and add the carrot, turnip, leek and potato. Sauté gently for about 10 minutes or until softened.

2. Stir in the stock, tomatoes, bay leaf, savory or marjoram, soup pasta and salt and pepper. Bring gently to the boil then reduce the heat and simmer gently for 20 minutes.

3. Add the beans and okra and cook for a further 10 minutes. Finally add the sweetcorn, peas and parsley. Cook for another 5 minutes before serving.

TIME: Preparation takes about 20 minutes, cooking time is about 45 minutes.

PREPARATION: If preferred, add 175g/6oz fresh tomatoes and 75ml/5 tbsps vegetable stock or water instead.

VARIATION: Use any combination of vegetables in season to vary this soup.

PASTA, PEAS AND PEPPERS

This very colourful salad is simple, but is substantial enough to be a meal in itself.

SERVES 2

120g/4oz mixed, plain and wholemeal pasta shells
Salt
120g/4oz frozen peas
½ green pepper, sliced
½ red pepper, sliced
½ yellow pepper, sliced
75ml/5 tbsps vegetable or olive oil
2 tbsps white wine vinegar
½ tbsp Dijon or wholegrain mustard
1 tsp poppy seeds
1 tsp chopped fresh parsley
½ tsp chopped fresh thyme
Freshly ground black pepper
2 spring onions, shredded
60g/2oz vegetarian Cheddar cheese, finely grated

1. Cook the pasta in plenty of lightly salted boiling water for 10 minutes until 'al dente' or as directed on the packet.

2. Drain the pasta and cool under running cold water. When cold drain well.

3. Cook the peas and peppers in boiling water for 5 minutes. Drain and add to the pasta.

4. Place the oil, vinegar, mustard, poppy seeds, herbs and a little seasoning in a bowl and whisk vigorously until the dressing is thick and pale coloured.

5. Pour the dressing over the pasta. Toss well and chill in the refrigerator.

6. Stir the spring onions and cheese into the salad and serve immediately.

TIME: Preparation takes about 15 minutes, plus chilling. Cooking takes about 20 minutes.

VARIATION: Use 30g/1oz salted peanuts instead of cheese in this recipe.

Butter Bean One-Pot

This is a quick to make, all-in-one supper dish.

SERVES 2

1 tbsp vegetable oil
½ green pepper, finely chopped
1 small onion, finely chopped
1 stick celery, diced
175g/6oz canned tomatoes
1 large potato, peeled and diced
140ml/¼ pint vegetable stock or water
1 tbsp finely chopped parsley
Salt and pepper
225g/8oz cooked butter beans

1. Heat the oil in a pan, then add the pepper, onion and celery and sauté until the onion begins to brown.

2. Add the tomatoes and their juice, plus the potato, stock, parsley, salt and pepper.

3. Simmer for about 30 minutes or until the liquid is reduced by half.

4. Add the beans and heat through gently for 5-10 minutes.

TIME: Preparation takes about 15 minutes, cooking takes 50 minutes.

SERVING IDEAS: Serve with lots of crusty bread. Garlic bread also goes well with this dish.

VARIATION: To make a more substantial main course dish, follow the recipe to the end of instruction 3. Add the beans and stir well. Place in a casserole dish, top with a crumble mixture and bake in a hot oven for 25 minutes.

Watercress Stuffed Potatoes

An unusual and delicious way of serving this popular vegetable meal.

SERVES 2

2 large baking potatoes, scrubbed
2 eggs
30g/1oz butter or vegetable margarine
60g/2oz button mushrooms, sliced
1 shallot, finely chopped
25g/¾ oz plain flour
200ml/7 fl oz milk
30g/1oz vegetarian Cheddar cheese, grated
Pinch dry mustard
Pinch cayenne pepper
Salt and freshly ground black pepper
½ bunch watercress, chopped
Grated cheese, cayenne pepper and
    watercress sprigs, to garnish

1. Prick the potatoes a few times with a fork and place them directly on the shelf of an oven preheated to 200°C/400°F/Gas Mark 6. Bake for ¾-1 hour, depending on the size, or until they are soft when squeezed. Reduce the oven temperature to 160°C/325°F/Gas Mark 3 and keep potatoes warm whilst completing the dish.

2. Poach the eggs in gently simmering water for 3½-5 minutes, or until the white and yolk is just set. Remove from the pan and keep in cold water until required.

3. Melt half of the butter in a small pan and sauté the mushrooms and shallot for 5 minutes until just beginning to soften.

4. Melt the remaining butter, stir in the flour and cook for about 1 minute. Remove from the heat and gradually add 140ml/ ¼ pint of the milk, stirring well after each addition. Return to the heat and bring to the boil, then cook gently until the sauce thickens. Stir in the cheese, mustard, cayenne and salt and pepper, and continue cooking until the cheese melts.

5. When the potatoes are cooked, cut a slice off the top and scoop out the flesh with a spoon, taking care to leave a border inside each skin to form a firm shell.

6. Divide the mushroom mixture between the potatoes and top with a well drained egg. Spoon the cheese sauce mixture over the top.

7. Heat the remaining milk until almost boiling. Mash the potato flesh, then gradually beat in the hot milk and watercress. Pipe or spoon the potato over the sauce in the potato shell.

8. Sprinkle the top with a little extra cheese and return to the oven for 15 minutes to warm through. Serve garnished with a sprinkling of cayenne pepper and sprigs of watercress.

TIME: Preparation takes about 20 minutes, cooking takes about 1½ hours.
SERVING IDEAS: Serve with coleslaw or any other salad.

SPINACH AND PEPPER CASSEROLE

This hearty, warm casserole makes a substantial lunch or supper dish.

SERVES 2

225g/8oz spinach, washed, trimmed and
    roughly chopped
1 tbsp oil
½ red pepper, sliced
½ green pepper, sliced
2 sticks celery, trimmed and thinly sliced
1 onion, finely chopped
15g/½oz sultanas
Pinch of paprika
Pinch of sugar
Pinch of ground cinnamon
Salt
1 tbsp tomato purée
½ tsp cornflour
15g/½oz vegetarian Cheddar cheese
1 tbsp fresh breadcrumbs

1. Cook the spinach in a covered pan until just wilted with just the water that clings to the leaves after washing.

2. Drain the spinach well, reserving the cooking liquid to make the sauce.

3. Heat the oil in a frying pan and sauté the peppers, celery and onion for about 10 minutes, or until softened.

4. Mix together the sultanas, paprika, sugar, cinnamon, salt, tomato purée and cornflour. Make the reserved cooking liquid up to 75ml/5 tbsps and add to the cornflour mixture.

5. Add to the vegetables and cook, stirring until the sauce thickens.

6. Pile into a flameproof casserole dish. Mix together the cheese and breadcrumbs and sprinkle over the vegetables. Place under a preheated grill until the cheese melts and the crumbs are golden.

TIME: Preparation takes about 15 minutes, cooking time is about 20 minutes.

SERVING IDEA: Serve with a rice salad and a mixed leaf salad.

EGG CURRY

Quick and easy, this curry is a delicious way of serving hard-boiled eggs.

SERVES 2

2-4 eggs
1 small onion
1 tbsp oil
2.5cm/1-inch stick cinnamon
1 bay leaf
2 green cardamom pods
3 cloves
½ tsp garlic paste
½ tsp ginger paste
½ tsp ground coriander
½ tsp ground cumin
¼ tsp ground turmeric
½ tsp garam masala
½ tsp chilli powder
175g/6oz canned tomatoes, crushed
Salt to taste
120ml/4 fl oz water or vegetable stock
1 sprig fresh coriander
1 green chilli

1. Hard-boil the eggs in boiling water for 8-10 minutes. Cool them completely in cold water, then remove the shells.

2. Chop the onion finely. Heat the oil in a large saucepan and sauté the onion gently for 2-3 minutes until it is soft but not browned.

3. Add the cinnamon, bay leaf, cardamoms and cloves and fry for 1 minute. Stir in the ginger and garlic pastes. Add the coriander, cumin, turmeric, garam masala and chilli powder. Stir together well and fry for 30 seconds.

4. Add the canned tomatoes and salt to the spices. Stir in well and simmer for 5 minutes. Add the water or stock, and bring the mixture to the boil.

5. Put the eggs into the curry sauce and simmer for 10-12 minutes.

6. Chop the coriander leaves and the chilli finely, and sprinkle them over the cooked eggs to garnish.

TIME: Preparation takes about 10 minutes, and cooking takes 20 minutes.

PREPARATION: If a milder curry is preferred, reduce the amount of chilli powder to ¼ tsp and carefully remove the seeds from the green chilli before you chop it.

WATCHPOINT: Great care must be taken when preparing chillies. Try not to get juice into the eyes or mouth. If this should happen rinse well with lots of cold water.

SERVING IDEAS: Serve with plain boiled rice.

POTATO NESTS

An ideal supper dish and an excellent way of using up leftover cooked potatoes.

SERVES 2

1 small onion, finely chopped
460g/1lb potatoes, cooked in their skins
A little milk
Knob of butter
Seasoning
2 eggs
30g/1oz vegetarian cheese, grated

1. Cook the onion in a little water until softened. Drain.

2. Peel the cooked potatoes and mash them with the milk, butter and seasoning.

3. Add the drained onion and mix well.

4. Divide the mixture into two and shape into 'nests' on a greased baking sheet.

5. Crack an egg into each nest and sprinkle with the grated cheese.

6. Bake in an oven preheated to 200°C/400°F/Gas Mark 6, for 20-25 minutes or until the eggs are set.

TIME: Preparation takes 10 minutes, cooking takes 25-30 minutes.

SERVING IDEAS: Garnish with parsley and serve with beans and grilled tomatoes or a salad.

VARIATION: The nests may be filled with chopped leftover nut roast mixed with a mushroom or tomato sauce and a few freshly chopped herbs.

BEANS WITH TREE EARS AND BAMBOO SHOOTS

Tree ears are Chinese black fungi. These are usually sold dried and are available from most ethnic shops or delicatessens.

SERVES 1-2

3 Chinese tree ears, broken into small
    pieces
1 piece whole canned bamboo shoot
1 tbsp vegetable or olive oil
175g/6oz green beans, trimmed
1 tsp cornflour
1 tbsp soy sauce
60ml/4 tbsps vegetable stock
Dash sesame oil
Salt and freshly ground black pepper

1. Put the tree ears in a bowl and pour over enough hot water to cover them and allow to stand for 30 minutes.

2. Slice the bamboo shoot and cut into thin triangular pieces with a sharp knife.

3. Heat the oil in a wok or large frying pan and stir-fry the beans and bamboo shoots for 2-3 minutes.

4. Stir in the drained tree ears and stir-fry for another 2-3 minutes.

5. Mix together the cornflour and soy sauce, then stir in the stock, add to the pan and stir-fry until sauce thickens.

6. Add a dash of sesame seed oil and season with salt and pepper. Serve immediately.

TIME: Preparation takes about 20 minutes, plus soaking. Cooking time is 6-8 minutes.

SERVING IDEAS: Serve with boiled rice, noodles or a crusty wholemeal roll.

SPANISH BARLEY

Paprika gives this dish its distinctive taste. It is a colourful and delicious main dish which is equally good served hot or cold.

SERVES 2

175g/6oz barley
340ml/12 fl oz vegetable stock or water
1 tbsp olive or vegetable oil
1 small Spanish onion, chopped
1 clove garlic, crushed
½ green pepper, chopped
½ tsp paprika
Salt and freshly ground black pepper
225g/8oz canned chopped tomatoes
Tomato slices and chopped parsley, to garnish

1. Place the barley and stock in a saucepan and bring gently to the boil, then reduce the heat and simmer for 25 minutes or until the barley is tender. Drain and discard any excess liquid.

2. Heat the oil in a saucepan and sauté the onion, garlic and pepper until soft.

3. Stir in the paprika and cook gently for 1 minute.

4. Stir in the cooked barley, seasoning and tomatoes, stirring well.

5. Cook gently for 10 minutes until the juice from the tomatoes has been absorbed.

6. Serve garnished with tomato slices and a sprinkling of chopped fresh parsley.

TIME: Preparation takes about 5 minutes, cooking time is about 40 minutes.

TO FREEZE: This recipe will freeze well for up to 3 months. The flavour of the paprika will be enhanced during this time.

SERVING IDEAS: Serve with a tomato and basil salad.

VARIATION: Add 45g/1½oz pitted sliced black olives and 60g/2oz cubed vegetarian Wensleydale cheese.

CHEESE SANDWICH SOUFFLÉ

Unlike a true soufflé there is no need to rush this dish to the table as it will not sink. It is equally delicious served hot or cold.

SERVES 2

2 tsps wholegrain mustard
4 slices wholemeal bread
1 tomato, sliced
90g/3oz vegetarian Cheddar cheese, grated
1 egg, beaten
280ml/½ pint milk
½ tsp dried basil
Salt and freshly ground black pepper
Parsley sprigs, to garnish

1. Spread equal amounts of mustard over two slices of the bread.

2. Arrange the tomato slices over the mustard bread and sprinkle with the grated cheese.

3. Use the remaining two slices to cover the cheese.

4. Place the cheese and tomato sandwiches in a shallow dish into which they will just fit.

5. Beat together the egg, milk and basil, seasoning well. Pour over the bread, leave to stand for 30 minutes to allow the bread to soak up the milk mixture.

6. Bake in an oven preheated to 180°C/350°F/Gas Mark 4, for 40-45 minutes or until the milk mixture is set. Serve garnished with sprigs of parsley.

TIME: Preparation takes about 10 minutes, plus standing. Cooking time is about 45 minutes.

SERVING IDEAS: Serve with braised mushrooms or fennel.

VARIATION: Use slices of Spanish onion in place of the tomato and vegetarian Stilton in place of the Cheddar cheese.

GARBURE

This thick, tasty French country stew makes a warming lunch or supper dish. It is also an excellent source of protein.

SERVES 2

120g/4oz haricot beans, soaked overnight
1 tbsp vegetable oil
1 medium potato, scrubbed and diced
2 carrots, peeled and sliced
1 leek, washed and chopped
½ tsp dried marjoram
½ tsp dried thyme
½ tsp paprika
420ml/¾ pint vegetable stock
Salt and freshly ground black pepper
½ small cabbage, finely shredded

1. Drain the beans and place in a saucepan with enough fresh water to cover them by 2.5cm/1 inch. Bring to the boil, boil rapidly for 10 minutes, then reduce the heat and simmer gently for 1 hour or until the beans are tender.

2. Drain and set aside until required.

3. Heat the oil and sauté the potato, carrots and leek for 5 minutes. Stir in the herbs and paprika and cook for 1 minute. Add the beans and vegetable stock and simmer gently for 20 minutes.

4. Stir the bean mixture and season to taste. Scatter the shredded cabbage over the beans, cover and continue cooking for 15-20 minutes or until the cabbage is cooked.

TIME: Preparation takes about 20 minutes, plus soaking. Cooking takes about 1 hour 40 minutes.

SERVING IDEAS: Serve ladled over thick slices of wholemeal bread.

PREPARATION: Great care must be taken when cooking any dried beans. They should be well soaked, preferably overnight, then thoroughly cooked with at least 10 minutes rapid boiling before being eaten.

IMAM BAYILDI

Imam Bayildi means 'the priest has fainted'. Apparently the dish was so delicious that the priest fainted with delight!

SERVES 2

1 large aubergine
Salt
75ml/5 tbsps olive oil
1 onion, finely chopped
1 clove garlic, crushed
1 medium tomato, skinned and chopped
¼ tsp mixed spice
2 tsps lemon juice
½ tsp brown sugar
1 tbsp chopped parsley
1 tbsp pine nuts
Salt and pepper

1. Halve the aubergine lengthways and scoop out the flesh with a sharp knife leaving a substantial shell so it does not disintegrate when cooked.

2. Sprinkle the shells with salt and leave upside down on a plate for 30 minutes to drain away any bitter juices.

3. Meanwhile, heat 2 tbsps of the oil in a saucepan and sauté the onion and garlic until just softened.

4. Add the scooped out aubergine flesh, tomato, mixed spice, lemon juice, sugar, parsley, pine nuts and a little seasoning.

5. Simmer for about 20 minutes until the mixture has thickened.

6. Thoroughly rinse and dry the aubergine shells and spoon the filling into the halves.

7. Place side by side in a buttered ovenproof dish.

8. Mix the remaining oil with 75ml/5 tbsps water and a little seasoning.

9. Pour around the aubergines and bake in an oven preheated to 180°C/350°F/Gas Mark 4, for 30-40 minutes or until completely tender.

TIME: Preparation takes 25 minutes, cooking takes 1 hour.

SERVING IDEAS: Serve hot or cold garnished with fresh herbs and accompanied by chunks of wholemeal bread. If serving cold, chill for at least 2 hours before serving.

Mushroom Curry

An ideal snack or supper dish.

SERVES 2

120g/4oz leeks, finely sliced
1 clove garlic, crushed
¼ tsp grated ginger
1 tsp curry powder
½ tsp garam masala
1 tbsp oil
225g/8oz mushrooms, cut into quarters
60g/2oz creamed coconut, grated
2 tsps lemon juice
Cooked rice, to serve

1. Sauté the leeks, garlic, ginger and spices in the oil until soft.

2. Add the mushrooms and cook over a low heat until soft.

3. Add the grated coconut and cook gently until the coconut has completely dissolved, adding a little water if the mixture appears too dry.

4. Stir in the lemon juice and sufficient salt to taste. Serve on a bed of rice.

TIME: Preparation takes 15 minutes, cooking takes about 20 minutes.

SERVING IDEAS: Serve with a tomato and onion salad.

GRATIN OF VEGETABLES OLIVER

Fresh summer vegetables with a crunchy nut topping combine to make a substantial lunch or supper dish.

SERVES 2

45g/1½oz butter or vegetable margarine
120g/4oz black olives, pitted and chopped
60g/2oz dry breadcrumbs
90g/3oz vegetarian Cheddar cheese, grated
60g/2oz walnuts, chopped
1 tsp chopped fresh basil
Pinch cayenne pepper
1 tbsp oil
2 medium carrots, peeled and sliced
½ head broccoli, trimmed and cut into
    florets
120g/4oz French beans, trimmed
2 courgettes, sliced
1 red pepper, sliced
4 spring onions, trimmed
Salt and freshly ground black pepper

1. Melt the butter or margarine in a small pan. Add the olives, breadcrumbs, cheese, walnuts, basil and cayenne pepper. Stir to coat in the butter and set aside.

2. Heat the oil in a wok or large frying pan and stir-fry the carrots for 5 minutes.

3. Add the broccoli and French beans and stir-fry for 3 minutes.

4. Add the courgettes, pepper and spring onions and continue to stir-fry for about 5 minutes or until the vegetables are just cooked but still crisp.

5. Season with salt and pepper and transfer to a gratin dish.

6. Sprinkle with the breadcrumb mixture and place under a preheated grill for a few minutes until the cheese melts.

TIME: Preparation takes about 15 minutes, cooking time is about 20 minutes.

SERVING IDEAS: Serve with a hot tomato salad.

SAVOURY BEAN POT

Serve this exciting mixture with rice or jacket potatoes and a salad.

SERVES 2

2 tbsps vegetable oil
1 vegetable stock cube, crumbled
1 medium onion, chopped
1 eating apple, peeled and grated
1 medium carrot, grated
1½ tbsps tomato purée
140ml/¼ pint boiling water
1 tbsp white wine vinegar
2 tsps dried mustard
½ tsp oregano
½ tsp cumin
1 tsp brown sugar
Salt and pepper
225g/8oz cooked red kidney beans
A little soured cream

1. Heat the oil in a large non-stick frying pan. Add the crumbled stock cube, the onion, apple and carrot.

2. Sauté for 5 minutes, stirring continuously.

3. Mix the tomato pureé with the boiling water and add together with all the other ingredients apart from the beans and soured cream.

4. Stir well, cover and simmer for 2 minutes.

5. Add the beans and tip the mixture into an ovenproof casserole.

6. Cover and cook in an oven preheated to 180°C/350°F/Gas Mark 4, for 35-40 minutes.

7. Add a little more water after 20 minutes if necessary.

8. Top with swirls of soured cream and serve.

TIME: Preparation takes 20 minutes, cooking takes 45 minutes.

VARIATION: Use cider vinegar in place of the white wine vinegar.

VEGETABLES MORNAY

This simple but elegant dish will add a touch of class to your entertaining.

SERVES 2

120g/4oz new potatoes, scrubbed
2 small carrots, peeled and cut into thin
    sticks
1 parsnip, peeled and cut into thin sticks
60g/2oz mange tout peas
Salt
45g/1½oz butter or vegetable margarine
60g/2oz button mushrooms
½ tsp brown sugar or molasses
120g/4oz shallots or baby onions, peeled
25g/¾oz plain flour
½ tsp dry mustard
Pinch cayenne pepper
280ml/½ pint milk
60g/2oz vegetarian Cheddar cheese, finely
    grated
Freshly ground black pepper
Ground nutmeg, to garnish

1. Cook the potatoes, carrots, parsnips and mange tout separately in lightly salted, boiling water until tender. Drain and keep warm.

2. Melt half the butter or margarine and sauté the mushrooms for 4 minutes or until cooked. Remove with a draining spoon and keep warm.

3. Add the sugar to the pan, stir until dissolved, add the shallots and cook over a low heat for about 5 minutes, tossing frequently until soft. Remove and keep warm.

4. In a small saucepan, melt the remaining butter, stir in the flour, mustard and cayenne pepper and cook gently for 1 minute.

5. Remove from the heat and gradually add the milk, return to the heat and cook gently, stirring constantly until sauce thickens.

6. Stir in the cheese and cook until cheese melts. Season with salt and pepper.

7. Arrange the cooked vegetables on a serving plate and pour over a little of the sauce. Sprinkle with nutmeg.

8. Serve the remaining sauce separately.

TIME: Preparation takes about 30 minutes, cooking time is about 20 minutes.

SERVING IDEAS: Serve with rice for a main course or use as an elegant way of serving a side dish.

CURRIED CASHEW NUTS

The highly nutritious curry is simple to prepare and has a delicious flavour.

SERVES 2

1 tbsp vegetable oil
2 tsps white mustard seeds
½ tsp ground cumin
½ tsp ground coriander
½ tsp garam masala
1 small onion, chopped
1 small green pepper, chopped
90g/3oz cashew nuts, chopped
120g/4oz bean sprouts
30g/1oz raisins
225ml/8 fl oz tomato juice
Cucumber slices and coriander leaves, to
   garnish

1. Heat the oil in a large frying pan and fry the mustard seeds and spices for 30 seconds.

2. Add the onion and pepper and sauté for a few minutes or until just beginning to soften.

3. Add the nuts, raisins and tomato juice, stirring well.

4. Bring gently to simmering point and simmer for 10 minutes.

5. Add the bean sprouts and simmer for a further 5 minutes or until the sauce has thickened.

6. Serve the curry garnished with cucumber slices and coriander leaves.

TIME: Preparation takes about 15 minutes, cooking time is about 24 minutes.

SERVING IDEAS: Serve with boiled rice or mixed grains and seeds.

SAVOURY GRAIN CASSEROLE

This casserole serves as a complete meal for one person or serves two accompanied with lightly steamed vegetables.

SERVES 1-2

45g/1½oz brown rice
45g/1½oz split peas
1 stick celery, very finely chopped
1 small onion, very finely chopped
60g/2oz mushrooms, chopped
120g/4oz tomatoes, skinned and chopped
¼ tsp dill seeds
¼ tsp thyme
1 tbsp shoyu sauce (Japanese soy sauce)
1 small egg, beaten
60g/2oz vegetarian Cheddar cheese, grated

1. Cover the rice with boiling water and cook for 20-25 minutes; drain.

2. Cover the split peas with water and cook for 20 minutes until just tender but not mushy; drain.

3. Meanwhile, combine the celery, onion, mushrooms, tomatoes, dill, thyme, shoyu and the egg in a large bowl.

4. Stir in the rice and peas.

5. Place the mixture in a greased ovenproof casserole dish and cook for 45 minutes in an oven preheated to 180°C/350°F/Gas Mark 4.

6. Remove from the oven and sprinkle with the grated cheese.

7. Return to the oven for 10 minutes until the cheese has melted.

8. Serve at once.

TIME: Preparation takes 10 minutes, cooking takes 1 hour 45 minutes.

SERVING IDEAS: Garnish with a few whole cooked button mushrooms or grilled tomatoes.

SPAGHETTI WITH BEAN 'BOLOGNAISE'

Any cooked beans can be used in this recipe.

SERVES 1-2

175g/6oz wholewheat spaghetti
2 tbsps olive oil
120g/4oz onions, chopped
1 clove garlic, crushed
1 small can tomatoes, chopped and juice
    retained
60g/2oz carrots, diced
1 stick celery, sliced
60g/2oz mushrooms, sliced
½ small red pepper, diced
¼ tsp basil
¼ tsp oregano
¼ tsp nutmeg
1 tbsp tomato purée
140ml/¼ pint stock or water
90g/3oz cooked aduki beans
1 tsp soya flour
Salt and pepper
Vegetarian Parmesan cheese

1. Cook the spaghetti as per the instructions on the packet.

2. Heat the olive oil in a large pan and sauté the onions and garlic until browned.

3. Add the tomatoes with their juice, the carrots, celery, mushrooms, pepper, basil, oregano, nutmeg, tomato purée and stock.

4. Stir well and simmer for about 20 minutes or until the vegetables are tender.

5. Add the cooked beans and simmer for a further 5 minutes.

6. Mix the soya flour with a little water and add to the sauce, season and allow to cook for 2 minutes.

7. Drain the spaghetti and serve topped with the sauce and a sprinkling of vegetarian Parmesan cheese.

TIME: Preparation takes about 30 minutes, cooking takes 35 minutes.

COOK'S TIP: Add a tablespoon of oil to the water in which the spaghetti is cooked to prevent it from sticking together.

GLAZED VEGETABLES

*Using everyday vegetables, this delicious casserole is economic
and very tasty.*

SERVES 1-2

15g/½oz vegetable margarine
1½ tsps light muscovado sugar
2 tbsps vegetable stock
1 carrot, peeled and cut into sticks
1 salsify, peeled and cut into rounds
1 turnip, peeled and cut into wedges
90g/3oz pickling onions or shallots, cut in
    half if large
60g/2oz large mushrooms, quartered
½ tsp chopped fresh rosemary or thyme
Salt and freshly ground black pepper
1 tsp Dijon mustard
Fresh rosemary, to garnish

1. Melt the margarine and stir in the sugar and stock, stir until the sugar dissolves.

2. Add the carrot, salsify, turnip and onions or shallots and cook over a low heat for about 10 minutes or until softened, tossing frequently.

3. Add the mushrooms, herbs, seasoning and mustard. Cover and cook over a low heat for 10 minutes or until all the vegetables are tender, tossing occasionally.

4. Serve garnished with fresh rosemary.

TIME: Preparation takes about 20 minutes, cooking takes about 20 minutes.

VARIATION: Change the combination of fresh vegetables to suit the season
or personal taste.

SERVING IDEAS: Serve with wholemeal bread or jacket potatoes.

Sweet and Sour Nuggets

Almond nuggets, with the crunchy texture of water chestnuts are accompanied with a sweet and sour sauce to create a dish which tastes as good as it looks.

SERVES 2

15g/½oz butter or vegetable margarine
1 small shallot, finely chopped
15g/½oz plain flour
75ml/5 tbsps milk
30g/1oz ground almonds
30g/1oz water chestnuts, chopped
1 tsp chopped fresh parsley
1 tsp ground ginger
Beaten egg
Salt and freshly ground black pepper
Dry breadcrumbs, to coat
Sesame seeds, to coat
Oil, for shallow frying
30g/1oz light muscovado sugar
2 tbsps white wine vinegar
1 tbsp tomato ketchup
1 tbsp soy sauce
1 small can pineapple rings, in natural juice
15g/½oz cornflour
1 small green pepper, sliced
1 spring onion, sliced
30g/1oz canned bamboo shoots
120g/4oz bean sprouts

1. Melt the butter or margarine in a frying pan and sauté the shallot for 2 minutes or until softened. Stir in the flour and cook for 1 minute. Remove from the heat and gradually beat in the milk. Return to the heat and cook until thickened.

2. Stir in the almonds, water chestnuts, parsley, ginger and a little beaten egg. Season to taste and mix to form a thick paste. Chill well.

3. Divide into 8 and shape each piece into rounds with lightly floured hands. Dip each round into the remaining egg and coat in a mixture of dry breadcrumbs and sesame seeds. Shallow fry for 3 minutes on each side until golden. Keep warm.

4. While the nuggets are cooking, mix together the sugar, vinegar, ketchup and soy sauce. Drain the juice from the pineapple and add to the soy sauce mixture. Cut the pineapple into chunks and reserve.

5. Mix a little of the soy sauce mixture with the cornflour and heat the remainder in a small pan until just boiling. Spoon a little of the hot sauce onto the cornflour mixture then return to the pan and cook until thickened.

6. Add the pepper, spring onion, bamboo shoots and pineapple chunks and simmer for 5 minutes.

7. Arrange the bean sprouts on two serving plates and place the nuggets on top. Pour a little of the sauce over the nuggets and serve the remainder separately.

TIME: Preparation takes about 25 minutes, plus chilling. Cooking time is about 20 minutes.

SERVING IDEAS: Serve with salad and baked potatoes, rice or mixed grains.

MUSHROOMS FLORENTINE

This delicious way of serving large mushrooms is suitable for informal entertaining or for a substantial supper or lunch dish.

SERVES 2

75g/2½oz vegetable margarine
1 shallot, finely chopped
460g/1lb spinach, stalks removed, washed
   and roughly shredded
2 tomatoes, skinned, seeded and chopped
Salt and freshly ground black pepper
Pinch nutmeg
225g/8oz open cap mushrooms
25g/¾oz plain flour
¼ tsp dry mustard
Pinch cayenne pepper
280ml/½ pint milk
120g/4oz vegetarian Cheddar cheese,
   grated
Paprika, to garnish

---

1. Melt 15g/½oz of the margarine in a large pan and sauté the shallot until softened.

2. Add the spinach with just the water that is left clinging to the leaves, cover and cook for 5 minutes or until wilted.

3. Add the tomatoes, seasoning and nutmeg and stir to combine well.

4. Spread the spinach mixture in a shallow flame-proof dish and keep warm.

5. Melt the remaining margarine and sauté the mushrooms for 6 minutes, or until just soft. Remove with a draining spoon and arrange on the spinach.

6. Stir the flour into the pan and cook for 1 minute.

7. Remove from the heat and gradually add the milk, stirring after each addition.

8. Return to the heat, bring to the boil and cook, stirring until thickened.

9. Stir in 90g/3oz of the cheese and cook until it melts. Season with salt, pepper, mustard and cayenne.

10. Spoon the sauce over the mushrooms and sprinkle with the remaining cheese.

11. Flash under a preheated grill to melt the cheese. Serve sprinkled with a little paprika.

TIME: Preparation takes about 20 minutes, cooking takes about 20 minutes.

VARIATION: Wild mushrooms are now easily available and make a sophisticated alternative to the cap mushrooms used in this recipe.

SWEET BEAN CURRY

This excellent curry will freeze well for up to six weeks.

SERVES 2

90g/3oz red kidney beans, soaked
   overnight
15g/½oz butter or margarine
1 small onion, sliced
1 small apple, cored and chopped
90g/3oz mushrooms, sliced
2 tsps curry powder
15g/½oz unbleached flour
280ml/½ pint bean stock or bean stock and
   water
Salt to taste
2 tsps lemon juice
2 tsps chutney
30g/1oz sultanas
30g/1oz creamed coconut, grated or
   chopped

1. Drain the beans, put into a large pan and cover with cold water.

2. Bring to the boil and boil vigorously for 10-15 minutes, turn down the heat and boil for about 1 hour, or until the beans are tender but still whole.

3. Melt the butter or margarine and cook the onion until it is well browned.

4. Add the apple and mushrooms and cook for 2-3 minutes.

5. Add the curry powder and flour and cook for a couple of minutes, stirring all the time.

6. Gradually add the bean stock and stir until smooth.

7. Add the seasoning, lemon juice, chutney, sultanas and beans and cook for 10-15 minutes.

8. Just before serving add the creamed coconut and stir until dissolved.

TIME: Preparation takes 25 minutes. Cooking time, including the beans, takes 1 hour 25 minutes.

SERVING IDEAS: Serve with boiled brown rice and fried plantains – peel, cut into 1.25cm/½-inch slices and fry in hot oil until golden brown. If unavailable you can use unripe green bananas. Garnish the curry with quarters of hard-boiled eggs.

Vegetarian Shepherd's Pie

This pie will serve one person without any accompaniments and two people if served with vegetables.

SERVES 1-2

60g/2oz brown lentils
30g/1oz pot barley
200ml/7 fl oz stock or water
½ tsp yeast extract
1 medium carrot, diced
½ small onion, chopped finely
1 clove garlic, crushed
30g/1oz walnuts, roughly chopped
½ tsp vegetarian gravy powder or thickener
Salt and pepper
225g/8oz potatoes, cooked and mashed

1. Simmer the lentils and barley in 140ml/¼ pint of the stock and the yeast extract for 30 minutes.

2. Meanwhile, cook the carrot, onion, garlic and walnuts in the remaining stock for 15 minutes, or until tender.

3. Mix the gravy powder or thickener with a little water, add to the carrot mixture and stir over a low heat until thickened.

4. Combine the lentils and barley with the carrot mixture, season and place in an ovenproof dish.

5. Cover with the mashed potato and cook in an oven preheated to 180°C/350°F/Gas Mark 4, for about 30 minutes until browned on top.

TIME: Preparation takes 15 minutes, cooking takes 1 hour.

SERVING IDEAS: Garnish with grilled tomatoes and serve with vegetables in season – broccoli, sprouts, spring cabbage etc.

Japanese Steamer

The Japanese are renowned for their elegant cuisine and this simple to prepare recipe is no exception.

SERVES 2

60g/2oz buckwheat noodles
8 dried shiitake mushrooms, soaked
   overnight
60g/2oz button mushrooms
4 baby corn cobs, sliced lengthways
½ small daikon (mooli) radish, sliced
175g/6oz tofu, drained and cut into chunks
½ packet dried sea spinach, soaked for 1
   hour
75ml/5 tbsps Japanese soy sauce
Small piece fresh root ginger, peeled and
   grated
2 tbsps vegetable stock
2 tsps sherry
½ tsp cornflour
Lemon slices and fresh chives, to garnish

1. Cook the noodles in plenty of lightly salted, boiling water for 10 minutes.

2. Remove the stems from the shiitake mushroooms and discard. Steam the mushroom caps, button mushrooms, baby corn and diakon for 5-10 minutes.

3. Steam the tofu and sea spinach for 2 minutes.

4. Make the sauce by heating the soy sauce, ginger and vegetable stock in a small pan until simmering.

5. Blend the sherry and cornflour together and add to the pan. Cook until thickened.

6. Drain the noodles and arrange with the steamed vegetable on serving plates.

7. Pour a little of the sauce over each and serve the remaining sauce separately. Garnish with lemon slices and chives.

TIME: Preparation takes about 30 minutes, plus soaking. Cooking takes about 15 minutes.

PREPARATION: Prepare the ingredients in the order specified, so that they are all cooked at the same time.

Sweet Potato and French Bean Pasties

These pasties are a tasty addition to any lunch box or picnic basket.

SERVES 2

½ small onion, finely chopped
1 clove garlic, crushed
1 tbsp oil
¼ tsp freshly grated ginger
¼ tsp chilli powder
Large pinch turmeric
¼ tsp ground cumin
½ tsp ground coriander
Large pinch mustard powder
1 small sweet potato, cooked and finely
    diced
60g/2oz French beans, chopped into
    1.2cm/½-inch lengths
1 tbsp water or stock
Salt and pepper
120g/4oz wholemeal shortcrust pastry

1. Sauté the onion and garlic in the oil until soft.

2. Add the ginger and all the spices and stir.

3. Add the diced potato, beans and water or stock and cook gently for 4-5 minutes or until the beans begin to cook.

4. Allow the mixture to cool and season well.

5. Roll the pastry out into 2 circles.

6. Place half of the filling in the centre of each circle and dampen the edges of the pastry with a little water.

7. Join the pastry together over the filling.

8. Make a small hole in each pasty and glaze with milk or beaten egg.

9. Bake in an oven preheated to 200°C/400°F/Gas Mark 6, for 15-20 minutes.

TIME: Preparation, including making the pastry, takes 25 minutes. Cooking takes 15-20 minutes.

TO FREEZE: The pasties will freeze well for up to 2 months. Thaw at room temperature.

BLACK AND WHITE BAKE WITH BOULANGERE TOPPING

Serve this hearty dish with lightly steamed vegetables.

SERVES 2

60g/2oz black kidney beans, soaked
   overnight and cooked until tender
1 small cauliflower, divided into florets
400ml/14 fl oz water
1 bay leaf
140ml/¼ pint milk
1 tbsp sunflower oil
1 small onion, very finely chopped
25g/¾oz fine wholemeal flour
2 tsps wholegrain mustard
2 tsps parsley, chopped
Salt and pepper
175-225g/6-8oz potatoes, cooked and cut
   into 5mm/¼-inch slices
15g/½oz butter or vegetable margarine

---

1. Wash and drain the cauliflower florets.

2. Bring the water to the boil in a large pan, add the bay leaf and a little salt.

3. Plunge the cauliflower into the water, return to the boil, cover and poach the florets for 8-10 minutes, or until just cooked.

4. Drain, discard the bay leaf and reserve the cooking water.

5. Top up the milk with the cooking water to give 280ml/½ pint.

6. Heat the oil in a small pan and gently sauté the onion until soft.

7. Stir in the flour and cook over a gentle heat for 1-2 minutes.

8. Gradually add the milk and water, stirring all the time to avoid lumps.

9. Add the mustard and cook gently for a further 3 minutes.

10. Drain the cooked beans and return them to a large pan, add the florets and mix well.

11. Pour the mustard sauce over the beans and cauliflower and stir in the chopped parsley and seasoning.

12. Place the mixture in a greased casserole dish.

13. Top with the sliced potatoes, overlapping them slightly, and dot with the butter or margarine.

14. Bake in an oven preheated to 180°C/350°F/ Gas Mark 4 for 20-25 minutes, until the top is nicely browned.

TIME: Preparation takes 25 minutes. Cooking time, including the beans, takes 1 hour 10 minutes.

TO FREEZE: Freeze the base for 4-6 weeks and add the topping when required.

COURGETTE AND SWEETCORN SAVOURY

This is an excellent way to use up leftover pasta.

SERVES 2

2 tsps oil
1 small onion, chopped
120g/4oz courgettes, sliced
90g/3oz canned sweetcorn, drained
90g/3oz cooked pasta shapes
Pinch of oregano
2 tsps tomato purée
Salt and pepper

Sauce
15g/½oz margarine
15g/½oz wholewheat flour
140ml/¼ pint skimmed milk
1½ tbsps white wine
30g/1oz strong cheese, grated

Topping
15g/½oz wholemeal breadcrumbs
1 tsp sunflower seeds

1. Heat the oil in a frying pan and sauté the chopped onion until soft.

2. Add the sliced courgettes and brown lightly.

3. Mix in the sweetcorn, cooked pasta, oregano and tomato purée, and stir.

4. Season lightly and transfer the mixture to an oiled ovenproof dish.

5. Make the cheese sauce by melting the margarine and stirring in the flour to make a roux. Cook gently for a few minutes and then gradually pour on the milk and wine, stirring all the time, to make a smooth sauce. Bring to the boil, then simmer for 1-2 minutes.

6. Add the grated cheese and stir until it melts into the sauce. Remove from the heat and pour over the vegetable mixture.

7. Top with the breadcrumbs and sunflower seeds.

8. Bake in an oven preheated to 180°C/350°F/Gas Mark 4, for about 20 minutes, or until the dish is brown and bubbling.

TIME: Preparation takes about 30 minutes, cooking takes 20 minutes.

SERVING IDEAS: Serve with grilled tomatoes and creamed potatoes.

INDIAN VEGETABLE CURRY

A wonderfully tasty curry which has the added advantage of freezing well.

SERVES 2

Spices
1 tsp turmeric
½ tsp cumin seeds
½ tsp mustard seed
½ tsp fenugreek
2 tsps coriander seeds
¼ tsp chilli powder
½ tsp ginger
½ tsp black peppercorns

Ghee or vegetable oil (about 2 tbsps)
225g/8oz onions, finely chopped
140ml/¼ pint sterilised milk
1 tbsp white wine vinegar
225g/8oz canned tomatoes, liquidised with
    their juice
2 tsps tomato purée
1 tsp brown sugar
½ tsp vegetable bouillon powder or ½ stock
    cube dissolved in little boiling water
460g/1lb chopped mushrooms or mixed
    vegetables (e.g. mushrooms, cauliflower,
    carrots, potatoes, okra)

1. Grind all the spices together using an electric coffee grinder or pestle and mortar.

2. Heat the ghee or vegetable oil in a pan, add the onions and sauté until golden.

3. Add the ground spices, lower the heat and gently cook for 3 minutes, stirring all the time.

4. Add the milk and vinegar and stir well.

5. Add the liquidised tomatoes, tomato purée, sugar and stock.

6. Bring to the boil, cover and simmer very gently for 1 hour.

7. Add the vegetables and cook for 30 minutes or until tender.

TIME: Preparation takes 30 minutes, cooking takes 1 hour 30 minutes.

SERVING IDEAS: Serve with boiled brown rice, chappatis and Cucumber Raita – combine diced cucumber with yogurt, a little chopped mint, a pinch of chilli powder, cumin and seasoning to taste.

TO FREEZE: The curry sauce will freeze well for up to 3 months so it is well worth while making double the quantity.

TEN VARIETIES OF BEAUTY

*The ten varieties refers to the selection of vegetable in this exotic Chinese dish,
which is simplicity itself to make.*

SERVES 2

5 dried shiitake mushrooms

1 carrot, peeled

2 tbsps vegetable oil

2 sticks celery, trimmed and sliced
    diagonally

45g/1½oz mange tout

4 baby corn cobs, halved lengthways

½ red pepper, seeded and sliced

2 spring onions, sliced

30g/1oz bean sprouts

5 water chestnuts, sliced

30g/1oz canned sliced bamboo shoots,
    drained

140ml/5 fl oz vegetable stock

1 tbsp cornflour

1½ tbsps light soy sauce

½ tsp sesame oil

1. Place the mushrooms in a bowl and add boiling water to cover. Leave to stand for 30 minutes. Drain the mushrooms, remove and discard the stalks.

2. Cut the carrot into thin ribbons using a potato peeler.

3. Heat the oil in a wok or large frying pan and stir-fry the celery, mange tout and baby corn for 3 minutes. Add the red pepper and carrot and stir-fry for 2 minutes.

4. Stir in the remaining vegetables and stir-fry for 3-4 minutes or until all the vegetables are cooked but still crisp.

5. Add the stock to the pan. Combine the cornflour, soy sauce and sesame oil and stir into the pan. Cook stirring constantly until sauce thickens. Serve immediately.

TIME: Preparation takes about 15 minutes, plus soaking. Cooking time is
about 15 minutes.

SERVING IDEAS: Serve with boiled rice.

AUBERGINE ROLLS

This colourful and tasty dish is ideal when entertaining informally.

SERVES 2

1 large aubergine
Salt
1 tbsp vegetable oil
½ onion, chopped
1 clove garlic, crushed
225g/8oz canned tomatoes
1 tbsp tomato purée
Pinch of sugar
Pinch of dried oregano
1 bay leaf
2 sprigs fresh parsley
Freshly ground black pepper
About 3 tbsps olive oil
120g/4oz vegetarian Cheshire cheese,
    grated
60g/2oz black olives, pitted and chopped
90g/3oz vegetarian Cheddar cheese, grated
30g/1oz pine nuts
½ tbsp white wine
1 tsp chopped fresh parsley
1 tsp chopped fresh basil
Pinch nutmeg

1. Slice the aubergine into rounds, then lightly score the cut surfaces with a sharp knife. Sprinkle liberally with salt and leave to stand for 30 minutes. Rinse well and pat dry with kitchen paper.

2. Heat the vegetable oil in a pan and sauté the onion and garlic until softened, stir in the tomatoes, tomato purée, sugar, oregano, bay leaf, parsley and seasoning. Bring to the boil and simmer gently for 10 minutes.

3. Remove and discard the bay leaf and parsley. Blend the sauce thoroughly in a liquidizer or food processor. Push through a metal sieve to remove the tomato seeds.

4. Heat a little of the olive oil in a frying pan and sauté the aubergine slices, in batches for 1 minute each side, adding more oil if necessary. Remove and drain on kitchen paper.

5. Put the Cheshire cheese, olives, 30g/1oz of the Cheddar cheese, pine nuts, white wine, herbs, nutmeg and a little seasoning into a bowl and mix to combine well.

6. Spoon about half of the tomato sauce into a shallow ovenproof dish. Put equal amounts of cheese filling onto one half of each of the aubergine slices. Fold the other half of each slice over the filling and arrange in the dish.

7. Spoon the remaining sauce over the filled aubergine rolls and sprinkle with the remaining cheese. Cover with foil and bake in an oven preheated to 180°C/350°F/Gas Mark 4, for 20-25 minutes or until piping hot and the cheese has melted. Serve at once.

TIME: Preparation takes about 30 minutes, plus standing. Cooking takes about 40 minutes.

VEGETABLE COUSCOUS

Couscous is a popular dish in North Africa, where it is often cooked by steaming over an accompanying stew.

SERVES 2

2 tbsps vegetable oil
2 cloves garlic, crushed
1 onion, sliced
1 medium potato, peeled and diced
2 carrots, peeled and sliced
1 small turnip, peeled and diced
½ green pepper, sliced
½ tsp each, ground cumin, coriander, turmeric and chilli powder
425g/15oz can chickpeas, drained
280ml/½ pint vegetable stock
120g/4oz courgettes, trimmed and sliced
30g/1oz raisins or sultanas
30g/1oz no-soak dried apricots, chopped
Salt and freshly ground black pepper
225g/8oz couscous
2 tbsps natural yogurt (optional)

1. Heat the oil in a large saucepan and sauté the garlic, and onion until beginning to soften.

2. Add the potato, carrots, turnip and green peppers and sauté for 5 minutes.

3. Stir in the spices and cook for 1 minute. Add the peas, stock, courgettes, raisins and apricots. Season with salt and pepper. Bring gently to the boil and simmer for 30 minutes.

4. Meanwhile, place the couscous in a large bowl and pour boiling water over the couscous. Allow to stand for 15 minutes, then place in a steamer and steam for 15 minutes.

5. Pile the couscous onto a serving plate and serve the vegetables on top. Garnish with a little yogurt if wished.

TIME: Preparation takes about 20 minutes, cooking time is about 40 minutes.

PREPARATION: As is traditional the couscous can be placed in a steamer and steamed on top of the vegetables if wished.

MUSHROOM CROQUETTES WITH GREEN PEPPERCORN SAUCE

These tasty croquettes are served with a lightly spiced cream sauce and are sure to win praise.

SERVES 2

30g/1oz vegetable margarine
2 shallots, finely chopped
90g/3oz mushrooms, finely chopped
30g/1oz plain flour
120ml/4 fl oz milk
60g/2oz fresh breadcrumbs
1 tsp chopped fresh parsley
1 tsp chopped fresh thyme
Beaten egg
Salt and freshly ground black pepper
Dry breadcrumbs, for coating
Oil, for shallow frying
1 tbsp dry vermouth or white wine
200ml/7 fl oz double cream
4 tsps green peppercorns in brine, drained
½ small red pepper, diced

1. Melt 25g/¾oz of the margarine in a frying pan and stir in half the shallots and all the mushrooms. Sauté for 5 minutes or until softened.

2. Stir in 25g/¾oz of the flour and cook for 1 minute. Remove from the heat and gradually beat in the milk. Return to the heat and cook until thickened.

3. Stir in the breadcrumbs, parsley, thyme and a little egg. Season to taste and mix to form a thick paste. Add extra breadcrumbs if the paste is too thin, and chill well.

4. Divide into 6 and shape each piece into small ovals with lightly floured hands. Dip each oval in the remaining egg and coat in dry breadcrumbs. Shallow fry for 3 minutes on each side, or until golden.

5. Meanwhile melt the remaining margarine in a small saucepan. Add the remaining shallot and sauté until softened. Stir in the remaining flour, whisk in the vermouth or wine and cream. Season to taste. Cook until slightly thickened. Stir in the peppercorns and red pepper, and cook for a further minute. Serve the croquettes with a little sauce poured over.

TIME: Preparation takes about 30 minutes, plus chilling. Cooking takes about 10 minutes.

SERVING IDEAS: Serve with a watercress and orange salad, new potatoes or rice.

VEGETABLE CASSOULET

This warming vegetable stew is an ideal recipe for using delicious autumn vegetables.

SERVES 2

120g/4oz haricot beans, soaked overnight

2 tbsps vegetable oil

2 clove garlic, crushed

1 leek, washed and cut into 2.5cm/1-inch pieces

2 carrots, peeled and sliced

2 sticks celery, trimmed and cut into 2.5cm/1-inch pieces

1 turnip, peeled and cut into 2.5cm/1-inch pieces

1 bay leaf

2 tsps soy sauce

2 tsps chopped, fresh marjoram

Salt and freshly ground black pepper

225ml/8 fl oz vegetable stock

15g/½oz vegetable margarine

45g/1½oz wholemeal breadcrumbs

1. Drain the beans and place in a saucepan with enough water to cover them by 2.5cm/1-inch. Bring to the boil and boil rapidly for 10 minutes. Reduce the heat and simmer gently for about 1 hour or until the beans are soft. Drain.

2. Heat the oil in a large frying pan and sauté the prepared vegetables for 5-10 minutes until beginning to brown.

3. Place the cooked beans, bay leaf, soy sauce, marjoram and seasoning into an ovenproof casserole and stir in the browned vegetables and stock. Cover and cook in an oven preheated to 180°C/350°F/Gas Mark 4, for 45 minutes.

4. Melt the margarine in a small pan and stir in the breadcrumbs. Remove the lid from the casserole and sprinkle this breadcrumb mixture evenly over the beans. Bake uncovered for a further 30 minutes or until the breadcrumb topping is crisp.

TIME: Preparation takes about 20 minutes, plus soaking. Cooking time is about 2½ hours.

VARIATION: Use any combination of vegetables depending on the season.

SERVING IDEAS: Serve with jacket potatoes.

CAULIFLOWER AND OLIVES

Kalamata in Greece, where this dish is said to have originated, is an area well known for its black olives.

SERVES 2

1 small cauliflower
2 tbsps olive oil
½ onion, cut in rings
75ml/5 tbsps water
2 tsps lemon juice
1½ tbsps tomato purée
Salt and pepper
45g/1½oz black olives
1 tbsp chopped parsley

1. Trim the leaves from the cauliflower and remove the core. Cut the cauliflower into medium-sized pieces.

2. Heat the oil in a saucepan and sauté the cauliflower for 1-2 minutes. Remove to a plate and add the onion to the pan. Cook to soften and add the water and lemon juice. Bring to the boil and return the cauliflower to the pan. Cook until tender.

3. Remove the cauliflower to a serving dish and add the tomato purée to the liquid and boil to reduce.

4. Pit the olives, chop them roughly and add to the pan. Pour the sauce over the cauliflower and sprinkle with chopped parsley to serve.

TIME: Preparation takes about 25 minutes, cooking takes about 20 minutes.

COOK'S TIP: A bay leaf may be added to the water while cooking the cauliflower. This reduces the cauliflower smell.

VARIATION: Add strips of tomato pulp with the olives if wished. Green olives may be substituted for black.

SPINACH WITH BLUE CHEESE AND WALNUTS

This hot salad makes an ideal accompaniment to a rich meal.

SERVES 2

460g/1lb spinach, washed
15g/½oz butter or vegetable margarine
Pinch nutmeg
Salt and freshly ground black pepper
60g/2oz walnuts, roughly chopped
60g/2oz vegetarian blue cheese, crumbled

1. Remove any tough stems from the spinach and place the leaves in a large saucepan with just the water left clinging to them after washing.

2. Cook over a low heat for 5-10 minutes, until the spinach wilts.

3. Put the spinach onto a plate and firmly press a second plate on top to squeeze out the excess water.

4. Melt the butter or margarine in the pan and stir in the spinach along with the nutmeg and seasoning. Stir well to coat evenly.

5. Quickly stir in the walnuts and cheese, tossing the ingredients together lightly.

6. Serve quickly before the cheese melts too much.

TIME: Preparation takes about 15 minutes, cooking takes about 10 minutes.

VARIATION: Used diced tofu instead of cheese in this recipe.

SERVING IDEAS: Serve with nut roasts, vegetable cutlets or pâtés.

GREEN AND GOLD SUNFLOWER SALAD

This colourful salad makes a spectacular and delicious addition to a summer meal.

SERVES 2

1½ tbsps sunflower oil
2 tsps lemon juice
Salt and pepper
1 large ripe avocado
4 ripe apricots
75ml/5 tbsps natural yogurt
1 tsp honey
Grated zest of ½ lemon
1 tsp chopped fresh parsley
½ small buttercrunch lettuce, washed and
    separated into leaves
30g/1oz toasted sunflower seeds

---

1. Put the oil and lemon juice into a small bowl with the salt and pepper. Mix together well.

2. Cut the avocado in half and remove the stone. Peel, cut into slices and mix these into the oil and lemon juice dressing very carefully, taking care not to break them.

3. Cut the apricots in half and remove the stones. If the apricots are large, cut them in half again. Add to the avocado and dressing.

4. In another bowl, mix together the yogurt, honey, lemon zest and parsley.

5. Put the lettuce leaves onto individual salad plates and arrange the avocado and apricots on top in a sunflower design.

6. Spoon a little of the yogurt mixture over the salad and sprinkle with sunflower seeds. Pour any remaining yogurt dressing into a small jug and serve separately.

TIME: Preparation takes about 15 minutes.

VARIATION: Use segments of ruby grapefruit in place of the apricots.

SERVING IDEAS: This salad could also be served as a first course.

LEEKS PROVENÇALE

This classic method of serving vegetables is exceptionally well suited to leeks, as the flavours combine so well.

SERVES 2

3 leeks, washed and trimmed
Salt
2 tsps olive oil
1 clove garlic, crushed
2 tomatoes, skinned, seeded and chopped
½ tsp dried thyme
1 tbsp chopped fresh parsley
2 tbsps dry white wine
Freshly ground black pepper
Sprigs of fresh parsley, to garnish

1. Cut the leeks into 5cm/2-inch pieces. Cook the leeks for 10-15 minutes in lightly salted boiling water, until tender.

2. Heat the oil in a small saucepan and sauté the garlic until softened but not beginning to brown.

3. Stir in the tomatoes, herbs and wine and simmer gently for 10 minutes or until the tomatoes are softened. Season the tomato mixture with salt and pepper.

4. When the leeks are cooked, drain well and place in a serving dish, pile the tomato mixture into the dish and toss to mix. Serve garnished with a sprig of parsley.

TIME: Preparation takes about 10 minutes, cooking takes about 25 minutes.

PREPARATION: Drain the cooked leeks very well as they can hold a lot of water.

GREEN BEANS WITH MUSTARD SAUCE

This is an unusual way of serving these delicious vegetables, and makes the most of their flavour and texture.

SERVES 2

225g/8oz green beans
75ml/5 tbsps vegetable stock
Approximately 75ml/5 tbsps milk
15g/½oz butter or vegetable margarine
15g/½oz plain flour
½ tsp dry mustard
Salt and ground white pepper
Snipped chives, to garnish

1. Trim the beans and cut into 5cm/2-inch lengths.

2. Bring the stock to the boil, add the beans and simmer gently for 10 minutes or until barely tender.

3. Drain and reserve the cooking liquid. Transfer the beans to a serving dish and keep warm.

4. Make the liquid up to 140ml/¼ pint with milk.

5. Melt the butter or margarine and stir in the flour and mustard. Cook for 1 minute.

6. Remove from the heat and gradually add the stock and milk, stirring well.

7. Return to the heat and cook until sauce thickens, stirring continuously. Season well.

8. Pour the sauce over the beans and garnish with snipped chives.

TIME: Preparation takes about 10 minutes, cooking time is about 15 minutes.

VARIATION: Serve the sauce with other vegetables such as broccoli, cauliflower or leeks.

CARROT AND CELERY SALAD

This salad makes an excellent accompaniment for pasta and grain dishes.

SERVES 1-2

120g/4oz carrots
60g/2oz celery
½ red pepper
45g/1½oz walnuts
2 tbsps sweetcorn
½ tsp paprika
Pinch chilli powder
2 tbsps French dressing

1. Scrub the carrots and then dice. Slice the celery finely and dice the red pepper.

2. Put the carrots, celery and pepper into a serving bowl and add the walnuts and sweetcorn.

3. Mix the paprika and chilli powder into the French dressing and pour over the salad.

4. Mix well and refrigerate for 30 minutes before serving.

TIME: Preparation takes 10 minutes, chilling takes 30 minutes.

SERVING IDEAS: To serve as a substantial first course or as a light meal for one, add quartered hard-boiled eggs.

POACHED PEARS WITH RASPBERRY COULIS

This simple-to-prepare dessert is superb when lightly perfumed with the fragrance of fresh hyssop, but you can use cinnamon instead.

SERVES 2

280ml/½ pint water
60ml/4 tbsps clear honey
1 tbsp lemon juice
2 sprigs fresh hyssop or 1 stick cinnamon
2 pears
120g/4oz raspberries
½ tsp chopped fresh hyssop
Sprigs fresh hyssop, to decorate (optional)

1. Place the water and honey in a saucepan or frying pan and heat until the honey dissolves. Stir in the lemon juice and hyssop or cinnamon stick.

2. Peel the pears and carefully cut them in half lengthways with a sharp knife.

3. Keeping the stalks intact if possible, remove the core with a grapefruit knife or teaspoon.

4. Put the pears in the syrup and bring gently to the boil.

5. Cover, reduce the heat and simmer gently for about 10 minutes, or until the pears are tender. Chill until required.

6. Meanwhile, purée the raspberries and chopped hyssop in a food processor or liquidizer and push through a sieve to remove the seeds.

7. Sweeten the raspberry coulis with a little of the honey syrup, if required.

8. Arrange the pears on serving plates and pour a little raspberry coulis over each.

9. Decorate with sprigs of hyssop if wished and serve the remaining sauce separately.

TIME: Preparation takes about 20 minutes, plus chilling. Cooking takes about 10 minutes.

SERVING IDEAS: Serve with crisp dessert biscuits.

PREPARATION: The fruit can be puréed by simply rubbing through a sieve, but blending in a food processor or liquidizer first makes the job much easier.

CRANBERRY CRISP

Cranberries are often looked on as being a fruity accompaniment to savoury dishes. However, their bittersweet flavour is complemented perfectly by the honey in this recipe to produce an interesting dessert which you will want to try over and over again.

SERVES 2

140ml/¼ pint orange juice
120g/4oz fresh or frozen cranberries
2 tsps caster sugar
2 tsps cornflour
½ tsp ground cinnamon
30g/1oz vegetable margarine
225g/8oz crunchy oatmeal cereal
15g/½oz plain flour
2 tbsps clear honey

1. Put the orange juice, cranberries and sugar in a small saucepan and cook gently for 10 minutes, stirring occasionally until the fruit softens.

2. Blend the cornflour with a little cold water and stir into the cranberries along with the cinnamon. Cook until thickened.

3. Pour into an ovenproof serving dish.

4. Melt the margarine and stir in the cereal and flour, stir to mix well and pile on top of the cranberry mixture.

5. Drizzle the honey over the topping and bake in a moderate oven for 15 minutes. Serve hot.

TIME: Preparation takes about 10 minutes, cooking time is about 25 minutes.

VARIATION: Use this topping to cover any fruit filling.

SERVING IDEAS: Serve with fresh cream or a fruit purée.

Maple Syrup Mousse

If you really want to splurge on a special pudding, use pure maple syrup instead of the flavoured kind.

SERVES 2

90ml/3 fl oz maple flavoured syrup
2 eggs, separated
1 extra egg white
140ml/¼ pint double cream
Chopped pecans or walnuts, to decorate

1. Place the syrup in a small saucepan and bring to the boil. Continue boiling for 5-10 minutes to reduce the syrup by one quarter.

2. Beat the egg yolks until thick and pale lemon coloured.

3. Pour the hot maple syrup onto the egg yolks in a thin, steady stream, beating with an electric mixer. Continue beating until the mixture has cooled.

4. Beat the egg whites until stiff but not dry and whip the cream until soft peaks form.

5. Fold the cream and egg whites into the maple mixture and spoon into a serving bowl or individual glasses. Refrigerate until slightly set, and top with chopped walnuts or pecans to serve.

TIME: Preparation takes about 20 minutes.

WATCHPOINT: Be careful when boiling the syrup, since it can burn very easily.

BAKED CARROT CUSTARD

The natural sweetness of carrots makes them an ideal ingredient in desserts.

SERVES 2

225g/8oz carrots, peeled
75ml/5 tbsps water
60g/2oz pitted dates, finely chopped
½ tsp ground cinnamon
¼ tsp ground nutmeg
Pinch of ground ginger
Pinch of ground cloves
2 eggs (size 3), beaten
30g/1oz pistachio nuts, chopped
200ml/7 fl oz milk
Pistachio nuts, to decorate

---

1. Coarsely grate the carrots. Put in a saucepan, add the water and simmer gently for 5 minutes or until soft.

2. Add the dates and cook for a further 3 minutes.

3. Place the carrot mixture in a liquidizer or food processor and blend to make a fine purée.

4. Transfer to a large mixing bowl. Stir in the spices, then beat in the eggs and pistachios.

5. Heat the milk until almost boiling, then beat into the carrot mixture.

6. Transfer to a shallow oven-proof serving dish.

7. Bake in an oven preheated to 160°C/325°F/ Gas Mark 3, for 40-45 minutes or until set.

8. Allow to cool slightly and serve warm, or chill completely before serving. Decorate with extra pistachio nuts.

TIME: Preparation takes about 15 minutes, cooking takes 40-50 minutes.

PREPARATION: Save time by using the grating attachment for the food processor if you have one.

BROWN BREAD CRUMBLE

The unusual crumble topping on this dessert is simple to make, high in fibre and very tasty.

SERVES 2

120g/4oz cooking apples, cored and sliced
120g/4oz raspberries
45g/1½oz fresh wholemeal breadcrumbs
45g/1½oz rolled oats
30g/1oz light muscovado sugar
½ tsp ground cinnamon
¼ tsp ground cardamom
30g/1oz vegetable margarine or butter

1. Arrange the apple slices in a small pie dish or two individual dishes and scatter the raspberries over the top.

2. Put the breadcrumbs, oats, sugar and spices in a mixing bowl. Mix together well to distribute the spices evenly.

3. Add the margarine and rub into the mixture until well mixed.

4. Spoon the topping over the prepared fruit and smooth the top with a spoon.

5. Bake in an oven preheated to 190°C/ 375°F/Gas Mark 5, for 20-25 minutes.

TIME: Preparation takes about 15 minutes, cooking takes 20-25 minutes.

TO FREEZE: The crumble can be frozen for up to 2 months.

SERVING IDEAS: Serve hot or cold with fresh cream or fruit purée.

VARIATION: Use the topping over any variety of prepared fruit.

CRANBERRY FOOL

A simple and refreshing dessert.

SERVES 2

150g/5oz fresh cranberries
2 tsps clear honey
60g/2oz whipping cream
90g/3oz Greek yogurt
Toasted almond flakes, to decorate

1. Rinse the cranberries and stew with a scant amount of water for 10-15 minutes or until softened.

2. Remove from the heat, add the honey and leave to cool.

3. Whip the cream and gently fold in the yogurt.

4. Combine the yogurt and cream with the cooled cranberries.

5. Divide the mixture between two stemmed glasses and decorate with toasted almond flakes.

TIME: Preparation takes 10 minutes, cooking takes 10-15 minutes.

VARIATION: As fresh cranberries may be available only at Christmas time, redcurrants would make an excellent summer substitute.